BOOK BENCHERS PUBLICATIONS PRESENTS

THE FEMINISM

COMPILED BY

SENITA F

AELAY PUBLICATION

A dream come true for every writers out there. We spot every possible problem for the writers, help in rectifying them and guide them towards the best outcome. We make sure to understand your needs, dreams and expectations, and nourish them with our services and stop not until we fulfill your dreams. The writers have a right and freedom to choose what they want here. They have us to guide them through the hardest path untill the end. Believe in us.

Aelay Publication - by a writer for the writers.

BOOK BENCHERS

Book Benchers is the affiliate of Aelay publication.
Both the publication is handled by Astro.
Aelay plays the role of publishing solo books.
And Book Benchers is epically for publishing anthologies.

Book Benchers have 2 different teams.

1. Tamil
2. English/Hindi

Never mind what our main motive is to help all the budding writers, who are seeking for their dream of publishing their own book to come true.

We are there to help out everyone.
In guiding for starting up with your carrier in compiling until finishing up your full book.

COPYRIGHT

(Affiliate by Aelay Publish)

Book: THE FEMINISM
Compiler: SENITA F
First Edition: Augest 2021

Published By:
The Book Benchers
5/175, Fathima nagar,
Kuthenkuly,
Tirunelveli -627104
Phone: 9944992571

Design And Executed by

ISBN : 978-93-5533-161-8
Page : 145

Acknowledgement

Acknowledgement is essential to boost up passion, making person more valid and precious, giving the team a great progress that makes worth.

We would like to use this opportunity to thank each and everyone who all the people involved in this book and, more specifically, to all the co - authors .Without your support, this book would not have become a reality.

We would like to thank each one of the authors for their contributions. Our sincere gratitude to all who contributed their time and expertise to this book.

We wish to acknowledge the valuable contributions of the Publication regarding the improvement of quality, coherence, and content. Last but not least, we would like to extend our gratitude to parents and friends who have been a huge support through the book.

FOUNDER

IRUDAGA ASTRO

Irudaga Astro, From Tirunelveli, Founder of Aelay and BB (Book Benchers)
He had completed his BE.
He has written 3 Tamil poetry book's which hits the top list on social media!
His main aim is to allow the writers to publish their words as their book rather than just Posting them on Insta.

LINK AND POSTER MAKER

CATHERINE ASMI T

Catherine Asmi T, From Tirunelveli
She has completed her M.com
Her passion is Drawing and Designing.

<u>TEAM HEAD</u>

She is a passionate writer from Chennai. Writing makes her pressure go away. She had played the role of co-author for more than 100+ Antho's.
She would like to thank her parents and her Loveable Brother for supporting her rather than stopping her from what she wanted to do! For being the main reason for achieving her dreams. As well as for standing beside her in all the ups and downs.
Whenever she feels like she needs to get out of her stressful timing or feels like she needs peacefulness, she starts to paint, she would never mind sitting in the same place for so many hours when it comes to her painting. She believes that anyone could hurt her, But never her books could!!

Catch her in Insta and FB
Insta: @theinnocentheart

FB: KA. PARINASRI

CONTENTS

- DISCLAIMER
- ACKNOWLEDGMENT
-
- COMPILER'S DESK

❖ SENITA F

- QUOTES

❖ ANOUSHKA KAUSHIK
❖ BIDISHA BHATTACHARYYA
❖ JEFLIN J.S
❖ KAVITA MODI
❖ LISPA DABHI
❖ NABISHBHA S S
❖ POOJA GANESHKUMAR
❖ PRATHIK KANTHARAJ
❖ RIYA GUPTA
❖ RUCHIKA BISWAL
❖ SNEHAL SHIVARKAR
❖ SUJI LISONICA C
❖ VARSHINI

- **POETRY**

* AADHITYA PRATHAM
* AHALYA MERIN A
* ANANYA P MISHRA
* ANKITA NAHAR
* ANNS FETRICA J H
* ARYA MURALEEDHARAN
* ATHIRA A
* CHIKUN PANDA
* BIBHUSMITA SINGH SAMANTA
* CYILRISHA A M
* DHARANI
* FAREEHA FAIYYAZ
* GOPIKA M
* HAR DEEPANSH BAHADUR SINHA
* HARSHITA VERMA
* JANANI KALAISELVI
* KANISHKA VARSHINI S.K
* KOMAL GOYAL
* MANISHA BASKARAN
* NAVEEN BHARDWAJ
* PREETHI EVANCHALINE S
* PRIYA B SINGH
* RASIKA SAWARKAR
* SABTECHA BELDAZER A
* SEWELL L FERNANDES
* SUGANTHI S
* SUNITA BAJAJ
* SUPRIYA C.S.K
* SUSHMA F
* SUTHAMANCHARRI
* TRIPARNA BISWAS

- SHORT STORY

- ❖ BERIL JEBASTIN
- ❖ KRUPALI MAKWANA
- ❖ NANTHINI R
- ❖ SANANSHIKA MALIK
- ❖ SAPNA.P
- ❖ TUSHAR R

DISCLAIMER

"THE FEMINISM" is an anthology enclosing a unique collection of Poetries, Short stories & Quotes penned by our Incredible and Extremely talented co-authors from various places. Our Editors have worked well at editing the contents of our Co-Authors and tried their best to find out the plagiarism.

All the Poetries, Short stories & Quotes were the unique & unpublished work by our Co-Authors. In case any plagiarism is detected, neither the compiler nor the publishers are responsible. The concerned Co-Authors are solely responsible for it.

ACKNOWLEDGEMENT

Our first and foremost thanks to our readers for picking up this book on having all their beliefs that this book could quench all the thirst they are seeking for in their learning process. Dear Co-Authors, our most sincere gratitude and profound appreciation to you all, because your part really stood as a keystone in bringing forth this masterpiece.

"THE FEMINISM" anthology provides various themes like Anti-Dowry Law, Feminist Perspectives on rape, A cry of a girl as well as various shades of emotions and longing for equality. In this Anthology the poetry follows quatrains as well as couplet. Some short stories were written based on the true happenings and the situation faced by every woman in their life.This work is contributed to the maximum by the entire family of "THE FEMINISM" Especially a big thanks to BOOK BENCHERS for making this book a successful one. Different Co-Authors from Various places have contributed their talents in writing and contributed their works. Last but not the least, We extend our warmest and endless thankfulness to the almighty, to our parents, to the whole family and all our friends whose presence alone gives all

COMPILER'S

SENITA F

Her name is Senita F. She is an English literature student from Kanyakumari District in the state of Tamil Nadu. She has Co-Authored many anthologies. This is her first Compilation work. Her charismatic aim in writing has contributed to her maximum level. She is very much interested in exploring her various creative writings that is presented to the readers.

To know more about her writing visit

Mail ID: senitapeter29@gmail.com INSTA ID: @iam_senita

The feminine

On hearing i am a feminine,

to take me in hand there was none,

it was like a funeral ceremony,

her support was only her daddy,

she is alive by her father,

and moulds her to a co-author,

Been reason for her smile,

he led her to walk more miles,

to stay healthy,

and to stay away from filthy,

a feminie is survived,

as her father thought her as a pride,

when everyone thought her as curse,

she turns her words into verse,

she doesn't ask justice for treating so,

she forgiven her foe,

and ties her with the fetter,

other teased and discouraged her,

her father encourage,

to break those fetters with courage,

-Senita F

Anoushka kaushik

She is an 18 year old girl who is from gurgaon and has lots of dreams in her eyes.

To know more about her writing visit

- ❖ Email: anoushkaushik08@gmail.com
- ❖ Insta Id: @Likh__awat

Book Benchers

- Real men are the reason for their woman's success.

- Girls are nature's strongest force, who can be the reason for your creation as well as your destruction.

- Women are capable of doing every single work which is present on this planet; she just requires your support.

- On what basis can you consider women weaker than men? They are the rock stars of every field nowadays.

- How ironic is this that people don't want to have a girl child but want a homely daughter-in-law.

- I don't understand why people always misunderstand the term feminism, what is their problem in considering girls and boys equal.

- Equality is the right of every human born in this world.

- I consider all men as beggars who ask for the dowry, are they incapable that they can't even give basic facilities to their wives.

- I don't know what today's men consider themselves, don't have a penny in their pockets and still w to rule over their wives.

- Feminism is strictly needed in our society so that our girls can fly high without being scared of someone who will cut off their wings.

-Anoushka kaushik

Bidisha Bhattacharyya

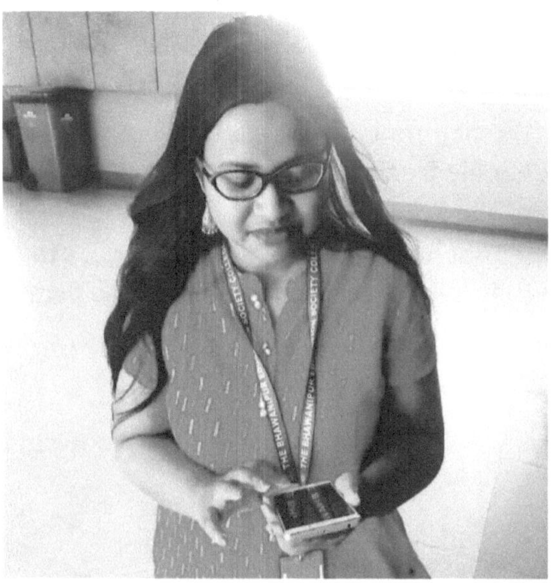

She is studying BA Honours in English Literature, 2nd year. She lives in Barrackpore, West Bengal. She has co-authored 25+ anthology books, two solo Quote books and one solo fiction book "Flash Pack". She has been awarded multiple times for her writing skills by companies like Awards Arc, Attainers Awards, Spectrum Awards, etc.

To know more about her writing visit

- ❖ Insta handled: @ lovewriting1
- ❖ Email: bidishabhattacharyya087@gmail.com

- ❖ Women's mission in life is to be successful, happy, peaceful and grow personally and professionally.

- ❖ Women belong to no one But to herself.

- ❖ Women no longer have to listen to others, she can live her life freely in her own way.

- ❖ It's not her fault that they hurt her, it's their fault, for how they have been brought up and the person they are.

-Bidisha Bhattacharyya

Jeflin J S

She is a budding writer. Currently, she is pursuing her bachelor's degree. She had decided to express her creative imaginations via short stories, poems and quotes. She is the co-author of many anthologies.

To know more about her writing visit

❖ Email: jeflinjose14@gmail.com
❖ Insta id: jeflin_14

Book Benchers

- ❖ Forget about respect, she deserves safety at least!

- ❖ Her fantasy life just changed as a nightmare, they just enjoyed her like a timeshare!

- ❖ She had no words to express what happened during that terrible, hilarious night!

- ❖ Her single drop of tears will tell thousands of untold stories!

- ❖ She suffered the pain only to show you light, still you try to put her into the dark!

- ❖ Her father gave her wings through his sweat and toiling hard work, but you cut it and did not let her fly!

- ❖ Every breath today you are breathing is only because of the pain she had suffered that day, just be thankful for that!

- ❖ Society will change when everyone starts to treat their own mother or sister or wife as equal as themselves!

- ❖ Just think a minute about your sister or mother before you are going to demolish a girl!

- ❖ If a girl stands for her own rights, the selfish surrounding guild will portray her as an arrogant, disrespectful girl!

-Jeflin J S

Kavita Modi

She met versatile personalities, Sampitroda, Moraribapu, puspendru kalindu, Raghuvir chaudhry, Kazal oza, Jay vasavada. Film director Haiderali, Kanvaljit. LateSuresh Dalal, Mrunalini sarabhai. Kanti bhatt. Chandrakant baxi… So many. She is Heroin, Nayika of short film, aavje vahali fari malishu. solodance of filmy song, solo acting of Kaikayi, winner in kavya pathan in shine your skill. Thera r so many videos on Facebook page, Youtube per. She is going to be a sachiveof Mahila shakha Gujarat ke liye Anter rashtriya hindi parihad me. Her poem on the whole process of consumer court has been published in Magezin upbhokta from Delhi. Publishing articles in Aastha, Samay, and Namskar Gujrat daily newspaper from America, Newzealand and in India, regularly. Articles published in Gujrati books named"એ મારી ભૂલ હતી " and other named "મારો શૈક્ષણિક અનુભવ" Compiled by Tathagat

To know more about her writing visit

❖   Email: kavitavmodi18@gmail.com

- ❖ We all are celebrating Women, everything changed except their safety and inequality.

- ❖ Not only the woman reached each corner of the world but the crimes too.

- ❖ Woman proves her ability equally though everyone restricts.

- ❖ A woman can become a father for her child efficiently, but a man can't become a mother for his child.

- ❖ A Mother awakes the whole night for her child, but a Father can't sacrifice as much as a mother does.

-Kavitha modi

Lipsa Dabhi

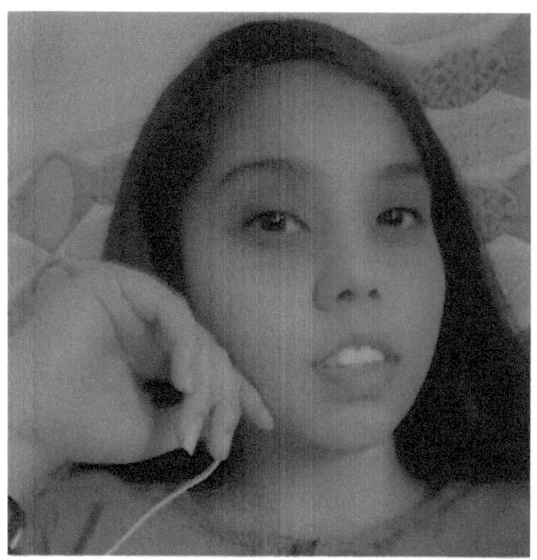

She is lipsa dabhi. She is an Author and also a good Co-Author. She is eighteen years old; she is a student of computer engineering. She is an extraordinary person. She is always a good leader.

To know more about her writing visit

- ❖ Email: lipsadabhi18@gmail.com
- ❖ Insta id: __lipsa__dabhi__0829

❖ A woman without a man is like a bird without feathers. You educate men but you don't care about women so your education is not as good. Respect to all women and respect to all girls, this is our priority.

❖ I hate men who are afraid of women's strength. Feminism is the radical notion that women are human beings; feminism is an obedient type of part of our societies.

❖ A feminist is a person who believes in the power of women just as much as they believe in the power of anyone else, respect to every person on life.

-Lipsa Dabhi

Nabishbha S S

Her name is S.S.Nabishbha. She is currently pursuing her bachelor's degree. She is a simple soul who believes in the goodness of this vicious world. She strongly believes that there will come a day in everyone's life where we could live unrestrained and also she loves to travel and explore new places.

To know more about her writing visit

❖ Email: ssnabishbha@gmail.com

Book Benchers

- ❖ Don't make a woman cry, God counts her tears.

- ❖ Expect women with love, not expect women with money.

- ❖ Women is a gift from God, Rape is equal to murder.

- ❖ Don't give your daughter's to Beggar, be a man standing against dowry.

- ❖ Crying doesn't mean that women are weak, it means that the woman has a heart.

- ❖ Be a woman, share your happiness, but always try to take away your pain.

- ❖ Girls are ready to be successful, but they are not ready to be failures.

- ❖ A girl who cries means, a girl who cares.

- ❖ If you make a woman laugh she likes you, if you make a woman cry she loves you.

- ❖ Feminism isn't about making girls strong, but in treating them equal.

-Nabishbha S S

Prathik Kantharaj

Prathik was a YouTuber with a pen name Prathik Kantharaj. He was also a blogger and orator. He had participated in more than 15 debates and 5 factual debates. He was a content creator and writer. Especially he loves to write Tamil and English. He has done several anthologies and done his bachelor art in Hindi. He was also a socialist and motivational speaker.

To know more about his writing visit

- ❖ Email: prathikkantharaj1209@gmail.com
- ❖ Insta Id: @ prathikkantharaj

Book Benchers

* She is a queen like a king who can do anything by her power.

* Women are not a toy to play; they are a part of life.

* Don't mess with her; she can destroy you by her firm.

* Women are not a headache to cure it by giving wealth or money to a shit called dowry.

* When there is an occurrence of dowry, then their society is considered as the hell of the earth.

* Dowry is not a key to running a marriage. Marriage is not a business; it is a turn where two similar souls combine.

* One can't sell her with wealth named dowry, she belongs to nature, and no one can sell without nature's permission.

* If asking for dowry is a crime, then giving it is also considered a big crime.

* Government and law can stop the dowry system, but only the society can put an end to it.

* The evil that we do against feminism will turn to us in another way, and that day is not far.

-Prathik Kantharaj

Pooja ganeshkumar

She is a Literature student, Writer as well as an artist, wishes to achieve for her family. And make her parents proud.

To know more about her writing visit

- ❖ Email: poojaganeshkumar295@gmail.com
- ❖ Insta Id: @Poojasathammai_official

- ❖ A girl who gets angry for everything. That's the girl who has lots of silent tears.

- ❖ The man knows to admire the girl's smile But doesn't know the pain of the tears.

- ❖ A woman is not a property to sell that is having the same responsibilities and feelings as men.

- ❖ A girl cries but that is not her weakness she comes back stronger.

- ❖ The fuel may doesn't burn sometimes But women's tears burn.

-Pooja ganeshkumar

Riya Gupta

Her name is Riya Gupta she is currently pursuing B.Tech from computer science and artificial intelligence. Writing always inspires her to fight peacefully for what is not right around us.

To know more about her writing visit

❖ Email: guptariya060702@gmail.com

❖ Insta Id:@ riyagupta_672

Book Benchers

- ❖ His being fat is a health issue; her being fat is a matrimonial issue.

- ❖ When she earns a good salary, she is dominating, and when she is a homemaker, she is illiterate.

- ❖ When she talks with boys, she is a slut, maintaining distance with them, she is so old fashioned.

- ❖ From throwing tantrums at her house, to facing all tantrums at in-laws, she grew up.

- ❖ If she doesn't speak she has an attitude, If she does then "Girls shouldn't speak this much.

- ❖ She took rounds with him along holy fire, Later she was burnt in same fire for not fulfilling their desires

- ❖ They give her life and they took it away, all in name of honour and values

- ❖ Biggest fear of women. Being on a lonely road and sound of footsteps following them

- ❖ We live in a society where we pack sanitary napkins in newspapers and black polyethylene bags, but alcohol and cigarettes are sold openly.

-Riya Gupta

Ruchika Biswal

Ruchika Biswal, a resident of Bhubaneswar, Odisha is a 13 years old writer and a voice artist. For her, writing is a hobby and she thinks writing helps you to forget the things which are not worth remembering. The words poured out of her pens' nib aren't just sentences, they are the carrier of a plethora of emotions, the carving solitude that drips from her life as a saturated sunrise..

To know more about her writing visit

- ❖ Email: ruchikabiswal120@gmail.com
- ❖ Insta Id: ruchikabiswal120

Book Benchers

- ❖ In laws people say they will keep our daughter as their own, but who else asks money to nourish their blood.

- ❖ They never act for her dreams but check the skin tone and beauty features along with the dowry just to give the girl a roof?

- ❖ Someone was right, he will admire you just to take advantage, forget your past, it will be the future, cherish the present but end up playing with the present, becoming the unforgettable past and Destroyed future.

- ❖ When a girl cries it's not her weakness, it can be the fire in her soul.

- ❖ A girl is the lost pearl in the ocean, after the oyster is left behind.

- ❖ Still I can't understand why the most beautiful creation of the creator is judged on the basis of skin tone and body structure.

- ❖ You don't need to be depressed about the dark tone, make the society realise by removing the tanned thoughts.

- ❖ A girl is a curse; a boy is a blessing because he will trade his surname in the name of dowry.

- ❖ A woman is the mirror of society, beautiful but dangerous when broken.

- ❖ A woman's tear is just not a piece of droplet it is the carrier of the frustrated life.

-Ruchika Biswal

Dr. Snehal Shivarkar

She is a doctor by profession. She started writing in 2019. She's here to become somebody; she'll surely be one day. Her Motto is to live life on your own conditions and never regret anything in life

To know more about her writing visit

- ❖ Email: snehalsaylee9@gmail.com

- ❖ Insta id: Snehalshivarkr

- She has faced rejection & has embraced them to lead the best life.

- She has come a long way from being called gossip queen to the leader of her life.

- She has come out strong listening to bad comments & then stopping them she shaped herself to get rigid, irrespective of asking for it.

- She's way more than you know her.

- She has made herself capable to oppose harassment and take a strong step for herself.

- She has made her way towards a dignified life.

- She no more needs a shoulder to cry, she rather might provide one.

- Women are now really strong; they aren't an easy deal to crack anymore.

- She has made a way from her darkness and has achieved light & respect by putting out a strong step.

-Dr. Snehal Shivarkar

Suji Lisonica C

Suji Lisonica C is an English Literature Student of Holy Cross College (Autonomous) Nagercoil.

To know more about her writing visit

- ❖ Insta handled: lisonica_03
- ❖ Email: lisonicaraj12@gmail.com

Book Benchers

- ❖ Every woman has a right to live with dignity.

- ❖ Don't be afraid to raise your voice against dowry.

- ❖ Every dowry demand is a Death threat.

- ❖ Accept women for their love, don't accept for their dowry.

- ❖ Don't sell your daughter In the name of dowry and marriage.

- ❖ Don't degrade yourself by demanding dowry.

- ❖ The man one who chooses his wife based on dowry will have a painful life.

- ❖ Women are born to live her life so, stop giving your daughters to beggars.

- ❖ The man one who makes dowry a condition to Marriage, he is beggaring not a man.

- ❖ Any women who suicide for dowry that is murder by a man.

- Suji Lisonica C

Varshini

Varshini was born and brought up in Tamil nadu, a 23 years old girl. The girls were willing to be a self made girl, dreaming to become an entrepreneur.

To know more about her writing visit

- ❖ Insta handled: @mymalon.world
- ❖ Email: varshiniblue1@gmail.com

- A woman is not a housewife; she recreates a new bond and relationship. Because she is a house maker.

- A woman is not a beauty doll, she is beauty with a brain.

- A woman sets tears to make it done successfully.

- We may not be physically equal, but try to treat us mentally equal.

- Though society tries to change your dream to a housewife. One man will always stand with you.

- A woman is not only a Queen to her king, she is a queen to her kingdom

- The Woman raised her voice not to just shout and stop. But to make deaf people's ears open.

- If someone asks what you can do, you are just a woman. She proves to them nothing is impossible for her to prove through god.

-Varshini

Poetry

Aaditya Pratham

Aaditya pratham is a student of Aditya Educational Institution, Andhra Pradesh. His first Alma Mater Sacred Heart School gifted him his aspirations, knowledge and skills. He aspires to be a Cardiologist. Science and Tech attracts him a lot.

To know more about his writings visit

- ❖ Email: aadityapratham05@gmail.com

- ❖ Insta Id: @aaditya.pratham05

Girls of light and dark world

Two girls once met by chance,

Both were looking each other with glance,

One belonged to the heaven's land,

Other had to suffer among Devil's wand,

Each got a chance to ask a query,

And God was there to make them merry,

First question was raised by a girl of light,

To make women's future bright,

Humans had many qualities in need,

And no one can have all that good-deed,

Though if you be a strong girl,

It is tough to live in this world,

Nurturance, modesty, empathy & affection,

Book Benchers

Were the qualities, god gave to a woman,

In case of men god gave the strength,

To protect the women every month,

Now it was the turn for girl of dark,

She was so dull and out of spark,

Why is our land full of misery?

And God wasn't happy to answer her query,

The strength given is now misused by some,

They dominate the women & rule over them,

This led to the construction of hell,

Thus the world became so miserable.

Now you decide the world you desire.

Cool and peace are now burnt in the fire.

The role you play is the teaching you give,

Not now but at least for your kids to live.

-Aaditya Pratham

Ahalya Merin. A

She is Ahalya, an Aesthete. She is an artistic writer who pens down her thoughts, dreams and desires vividly capturing petite details of daily life. She has a dashing personality, which enables her to spread hope and positivity through her fine stream of euphonious phrases.A tender soul who loves spending time with her cherished circles.

To know more about her writing visit

❖   Email: ahalyamerin17@gmail.com

❖   Id: @ms_meteor_shower_

Feminism

Golden, olden and here comes modern,

It's there without changing its turn,

There was time, women there on garden,

Paying their life in place of darken,

Four-walled room, with chained soul,

Just made their way with a control,

When you give them work to enrol,

Their life changed with ages in a scroll,

Why can't you digest, when they drive?

Do you think they are meant to strive?

Longing for love was their life,

Because, they promise to be your wife,

If their life was on your hand,

Don't make it as your demand,

Just make them live their best,

Without the knowledge that you suggest,

If you feel bad to accept,

It can be said to be the greatest theft.

-Ahalya Merin. A

Ananya P Mishra

She is a girl with a lot of patience and as calm as sea her name is Ananya P Mishra from Bhubaneswar, Odisha. She is completing her graduation in English Honors. Besides that, she is an Interior designer. Want to set an example for this era that inspires others and me as well.

To know more about her writing visit

- ❖ Insta handled: @ananya_payal 191

- ❖ Email: payalmishra2674@gmail.com

Let her fly

Though you push her inside out,

She comes up like a new sprout,

Holding a courage in,

She starts to swim with her new fin,

Having no one's support,

She needs no one to escort,

Travelling with her hope,

She climbs up holding the rope,

The society may try to change,

And often reminds you this is your range,

But never feel hurt,

Try to convert,

Book Benchers

If you try it,

You will never fall into the pit,

Let her fly into the skies,

Wide open her eyes.

-Ananya P Mishra

Ankita Nahar

She lives in AJMER, RAJASTHAN but heartily lives everywhere. She is very passionate about writing. She has always found comfort in words, and that is what attracts everyone. Writing is her therapy, she writes what she feels and experiences in her life.

To know more about her writing visit

- ❖ Insta handled: @ naharankita1
- ❖ Email: thegrtjainanki7@gmail.com

RAPE

How can one find happiness after rape?
A woman's life becomes a hazardous gap,
How do they get so much courage?
And putting her life in cage,

A man lives happily after spoiling her life,
But her life becomes a knife,
We can't change the past,
But can't let their future to be last,

And fight for their justice,
And change their thoughts wise,
They do with the pride of money,
We may not have money,

But we have a huge voice,
To shout for the wrong doings of a boy,
Never judge us by our looks,
We are more powerful than any books.

-Ankita Nahar

Anns Fetrica J H

She is Anns Fetrica, currently pursuing her master degree in English literature. She is a co-author of many anthologies. She is a dream catcher and all her dreams exist in her writing. Writing moulds her into a full fledged person.

To know more about her writing visit

❖ Email: fets1004@gmail.com

Rise up Queens

I render my thoughts for all of you,
Fortunately the change works for few,
I don't think this create a impulse of bliss,
But hopes to bring back all you miss,

I swear there is no stop for a crew,
Be united and give hands to flew,
Who gave the power to your pelvis,
Only you have it for not being selfish,

Come on queens rise and threw,
Don't wait for justice, just slew,
If you think something amiss,
Get out of the cage that resists.

-Anns Fetrica J H

Arya Muraleedharan

She is a budding psychologist, young heart in photography and pioneer writer from the motherland of Kathakali in god's own country.

To know more about her writing visit

❖ Email: chatterbox.wordpress@gmail.com

❖ Insta Id: _malupixels_

Tears fall apart

Friends yelled her slut,

When she talked with guys near the chestnut,

She was smashed by heart,

When the girls didn't give her the tart,

She feels bad because of her deed,

But what mistake she done indeed,

The words of the classmates made her cry,

But she just made a deep sigh,

Boys in the back row joked at her hairstyle,

They ministered to her like a reptile,

The girls again chanted about,

They gazed at her with doubt.

-Arya Muraleedharan

Athira A

Athira A is a young poetess from Ernakulam, Kerala State. She has completed her Bachelors in Science stream from St. Teresa's College, Ernakulam. She has been writing poems for 15 years as her passion. Book reading and reviewing is also her major hobby.

To know more about her writing visit

❖ Email: athiraorminnu@gmail.com

❖ Insta Id: _athira_a_

I am not a misandrist!

If I say women are the best,

Then you may call me a misandrist,

My dear friends I am not what you think,

I am the daughter under a man's wing,

And the devoted sibling of a man,

I can perceive the value and learn,

Never bear all his ill deeds silently?

Then I should define love as slavery.

Dear damsels, empower yourselves

To come out as stubborn warriors,

Who loves you too will fight for it,

It's the time to prove our wit,

Let us slay all with our flairs and glairs,

Let us forge a life of self love and cares;

I didn't write this only for my gain,

But to never let anyone labour again.

- Athira A

Chikun Panda

Chikun Panda is from odisha. She has completed her B.SC as well as LLB. She has worked with Tbss and Karvy as a business development associate. She has been writing since her school days.

To know more about her writing visit

- ❖ Insta handled: rhymergirl6

- ❖ Email: chikulpanda@gmail.com

Emotions of a Rape Victim

I was tied up with ropes,
And clear about my vision,
I wish to call the cops,
There is no one to listen,

I don't know why they kidnapped me.
I worried about my family,
My soul winnowed from my body,
I had no hope in anybody,

They enjoyed the every moment,
Seeing me shouting,
Seeing me breaking,
Seeing me trembling with fear,

Everything they enjoyed a lot
For a moment I thought,
As if I transgressed,
Being an employee I come to home at night,

As if I transgressed,
I had no bodyguard for mine,
As if I transgressed,
Is it my mistake being born as a feminine?

Book Benchers

Why couldn't they accept me as a woman?
Or at least as a human,
I cry and cry my tears are dry now,
If I see them I would ask them why?

My spirit is wondering here and there,
Just to get a true and honest answer.

- chikun Panda

Bibhusmita Singh Samanta

Writer Bibhusmita Singh Samanta writes motivational shayari, quotes, small poems about love, friendship etc... She believes that the girl, who laughs and talks a lot and seems very happy, is also the girl who may cry herself to sleep.

To know more about her writing visit

❖ Insta handled: @royal_princess_bibhusmita

❖ Email: purvaaa01@gmail.com

Cry of a girl

A girl-formed in foetus,
Further scanned for the reference,
If she is known as a - girl,
Made ready for her funeral,

Though she comes out of the womb,
Thought as burden and taken home,
Cry from her child,
Carries till she dies wild,

Brought up with - restrictions,
Which spoils her dreams of actions?
She is said what to wear,
Said not to go here and there,

Whereas - A girl is to fulfill their wish,
Don't teach her to do any dish,
Teach your sons how to behave,
His reaction from what you gave,

Girls are freedom less,
Until the guy's are punished to the best.

-Bibhusmita Singh Samanta

Cyilrisha A M

She is a simple soul who believes in the goodness of this vicious world. She loves to day-dream about stars and read books crazily. Nothing compares to the joy she gets when she spends time with her precious friends. She strongly believes that there will come a day in everyone's life where we could live unrestrained.

To know more about her writing visit

- ❖ Insta handled: @mag_da_leen

- ❖ Email: cyilrisha16@gmail.com

It'S Unfair

Book Benchers

Why do you confiscate her phone,

While it was he who device her fall,

Why do think she's always in danger zone,

When it was he who made her appall,

Why is only her virginity necessary,

While he treats a woman only as accessory,

Why is she a whore for replying to men,

While he flirts to women after ten,

Why is she supposed to endure,

While he always tramples her on the floor,

Why is rearing children and home always her duty,

While he is out having fun with a cutie,

Don't make her cry Give her a chance to justify,

It is so unfair but beyond that she wants to fly.

-Cyilrisha A.M

Dharani

She expresses herself through her words. Her thoughts are hidden in her quotes. She aims to be a famous upcoming writer. Her pen Name - Dharani Officially known as "Quotes Queen"

To know more about her writing visit

- ❖ Insta handled: @ Quotesqueen_iam
- ❖ E-MAIL: Quotesqueen.17@gmail.com

Value Her

She's Not Meant To Be,

Brought With Money,

She's Not Meant To Flee,

To Her Honey,

She's Not a Puppet that is,

Used For Your Emotions,

She's Not a Thing Or Biz,

Used For Your Reasons,

She gave birth to you,

She have equal Right,

She bore you too,

Of course she will fight,

Her lap is where you feel sleepy,

She's reason of your smile,

Hey you being creepy !

Stop stalking her profile.

She's not a movie piece,

To be with your all motions,

Never let her tears fall please,

She also has emotions.

-Dharani

Fareeha Faiyyaz

Fareeha Faiyyaz is a student and a writer who is deeply intrigued by the universe of emotions and feelings. Her writeups are reflection of her journey of self love

To know more about her writing visit

- ❖ Insta handled: @charmingfrequencies

- ❖ E-MAIL: charmingfrequencies@gmail.com

What does womanhood claim?

Words are none anymore,

Fight like a lion roar,

But way too rights still suppressed,

To stand in the society, lives crushed,

Fighting to get right to be alive,

To live safe we strive,

Like they achieved the suffragette,

Men became a threat,

To live a safe life and own rights,

To protect us from being sliced,

We express without ridicule,

Stop scolding women and change the rule,

Never let any innocent dismantle,

She is melting as a candle,

Why didn't women get independence?

Instead they were sentenced,

It is not their shame,

Instead a thing to be proclaim,

Let all of us put hands against those assaults,

Bring the change within their thoughts.

- Fareeha Faiyyaz

Gopika M

M.Gopika, a 20 year old girl hailing from Kadaladi, Ramanathapuram District. D/O: D.Muniyasamy-Mangaiyarkarasi, was born on 23 September 2000. She is a crazy writer and a budding artist. She performs many online and offline performances in poetry, Won more than 35+ certificates in poetry and Co-author of 20+ anthologies. She started her journey as a Tamil poetry writer a long time ago. But now she started her new journey as a English writer some months back.

To know more about her writing visit

❖ Insta handled: @ crazy_gops

❖ E-mail: gopika4041@gmail.com

Book Benchers
Not a feminist

I'm not a feminist,

Yet I help the females who needs her helps,

Females deserves to be a protagonist,

Her life is of huge steps,

In the form of my mom's life,

Their lives are like walking on the knife,

She sacrifice all her life-for her children,

Valuing them as a golden,

In the form of my wife,

This movement is a rife,

She sacrifices all her joy,

So now let them enjoy,

My daughter is a queen in my heart,

She never lets me fall apart,

I'm proud of my daughter,

And protect from every monster.

-Gopika M

Har Deepanshi Singh

He is Har Deepansh Bahadur Sinha. He belongs to Lucknow, Uttar Pradesh. He is a research scholar of Oceanography and has done masters in Geography from National Post Graduate College. He had completed his schooling from Study Hall. His hobbies are art, listening to music, cooking & loads of driving. His interest areas are Astronomy, Writing, and Photography & Travelling a lot.

To know more about his writing visit

❖ Insta handled: @Deepansh_sinha

❖ E-mail: hardeepansh.bahadursinha@gmail.com

Auspicious Her

She is a mother sister or daughter,

Extremely precious is her laughter,

Continuously works and looks after us,

Well she is completely marvellous,

She is the lifeboat of our lives,

If you want something she strives,

Accept her presence with golden arms,

By her smile the whole world charms,

Women need some love and respect,

And safety in few serious aspects,

It's our duty to make them calm,

Let's do this before buzzing of alarm,

Remember that she is also your wife,

Happiness should never fade in her life,

May god grant her a large existence?

On her we all are dependent.

-Har Deepansh Bahadur Sinha

Book Benchers

Harshita Verma

Co-author Harshita Verma is a writer from Lucknow. She has completed her graduation in commerce stream. She has been writing poetry for the last few years as her passion. She wants to be a novelist in future.

To know more about her writing visit

❖ Insta handled: @ 0___hsh

❖ E-mail: verma.harshita093@gmail.com

Plight of women

Social evils numerous which women are facing,

Innumerable the numbers are racing,

Commencing from the time she came into the world

Safe from female foeticide but unsafely unfurled,

From rude comments and eve teasing she suffers,

Travelling a tough task as touching occurs,

Growing up in an environment of male dominance,

Lost her freedom in early days a prominence,

Tears she has accepted in her fate,

Many suffering like her but no end to this gate,

Learning to accept it as her life is high

All she wants is to fly.

- Harshita Verma

Janani Kalaiselvi

Janani Kalaiselvi is from Salem district, Tamilnadu who is an upcoming writer. She was deeply in love with plants and flowers. She is a good writer who rarely does write ups which can be good poems.

To know more about her writing visit

- ❖ Email: priyakesavi25@gmail.com

- ❖ Instagram Id: @priyakesavi25

She, the Feminine

A best piece of Epic in my life,

In this great strife,

When I born into the world,

She never considered me to be hurled,

When I stepping out from her,

Mom- is all I prefer,

But when I got the phase of teen,

Forgetting how I must have been,

She's a Cup of Advice,

With words of wise,

Whenever I get confusions,

She remains for me as Solutions;

Book Benchers

Whenever I choose the wrong,

To correct me she remains strong,

Whenever I underestimate her love,

With her I always rove,

Whenever I sob in my pressure

She will be my only Refresher,

She is the most beautiful feminine in my life,

It may be common to the one who thinks it rife.

- Janani Kalaiselvi

Kanishkaa Varshini S K

S.K. Kanishkaa Varshini(22nd October 2004) is 16 years old and has interests in Writing and Art and craft. She looks forward to writing more and interacting with more writers around the world!

To know more about her writing visit

❖　Email: kanishkaa43@gmail.com

❖　Insta Id: kalon_poetess

Book Benchers
Powerful Tears

A girl never cries simply,

Or for being sincerely,

She shares her problems,

Not to inform you she is fallen,

She shares to relieve her pain,

Which was torturing her brain?

Sometimes girls won't share it,

And cries in the silent night,

Only pillows can wipe her tears,

Though there is no one to make her cheers,

She returns with the same power,

After many hours,

She is not going to leave it done,

Consoling herself 'ok it's gone,

She is going to fight it back,

To get what she lacks.

-S K Kanishkaa Varshini

Komal Goyal

Komal Goyal lives in Gharsana, Ganganagar. She is a 21 year old girl who is studying in LLB from Nehru memorial law (PG) College Hnumanghr. She writes about love,trust and many more interesting topics and some stories too.

To know more about her writing visit

❖ Insta handled: @ anika0510sharma

❖ Email: goyalkomal438@gmail.com

Worth of Women

A cruel tongue and a jealous mind,

Behaving as if you are a wild,

Void of pity and full of greed,

She judges the world by her narrow creed,

A brewer of quarrel,

Problem to tackle,

A breeder of hate,

Thinking every might be a fate,

Yet she holds the key to Society's Gate,

Strong woman holds it in the state,

They fight for equal pay,

Trying to encourage their way,

And Help us get on the track,

She'll be the same though you attack,

The woman who is strong and bold,

Is worth more than her weight in gold,

For she's the one when thing get rough,

To redefine the meaning of tough,

She is now born strong,

To change the world that is wrong.

-Komal Goyal

Manisha Bhaskaran

Manisha Baskaran has been composing her poems for more than a couple of years. She writes Poems, Book reviews, Write-ups and Micro tales. From her childhood, she had been shown her curiosity towards the language. She's fond of writing Essays as well. Her writings can be seen in numerous book collections, as she's a renowned author. Her educational background is in engineering, thus giving her a broad base facilitating many more topics.

To know more about her writing visit

❖   Insta handled: @ maniac_sha's poems

❖   Email: manishabaskar@gmail.com

Minerva

She may smile, for her family,

Hiding from her heart; a numerous agony.

She may or may not earn for her folk,

But she always works without any pock,

Our Society may deprive her tenacity,

But she'll lead her life with versatility.

She may sob in silence,

But never let her loved ones in menace.

Every woman's journey is distinctive,

But nevertheless, then an effulgent thrive.

She challenges every agreement,

But she'll never let you be in torment.

-Manisha Baskaran

Naveen Bhardwaj

Naveen bhardwaj a programmer by profession a lover of poetry maker and like reading books and audiobooks and he has telegram channel

To know more about his writing visit

- ❖ Insta handled: na.vin7832

- ❖ Email: bhardwajnaveen087@gmail.com

Courage

It's sadly for woman to experience,

The abuses in society,

Whether it is partner violence,

Or facing trouble living in unity,

The person she trust in their life,

Brings happiness in front of his sight,

Stands in times of strives,

And in the edge of lights,

Our social norms are like that face adversity,

Here and there the spread of diversity,

Holding unknown tag,

Roaming one place to another like a rag;

Book Benchers

Raise your voice against this campaigning

But didn't get any result for this happening,

To put this act to an end,

We climb up with courage and the magical wand.

-Naveen bhardwaj

Preethi Evanchaline S

Ms.Preethi Evanchaline is a budding poetry writer.She is an English teacher working alongside fun-filled and eminent team of students.She is a powerful force in the workplace and uses her positive attitude and tireless energy to encourage students to work hard and succeed.Preethi can be found reading books and writing poems , she owns a blog and she is a passionate writer.she is working as a co author of few anthologies.

To know more about her writing visit

❖   Email: preethievanchaline053@gmail.com

❖   Insta Id: @Pr.eethi97

Say you deserve it.

You are judged by your beauty,
Working for others isn't your duty,
Never fall so deep into an unworthy pit,
And you should rise up to say you "deserve it",

You are born not to impress,
Yet you should work hard to express,
Be true to your heart's commit,
And you should rise up to say you "deserve it",

Even when you are tired, don't give up,
Give your confidence an energizing syrup,
Be courageous whenever you get exploit,
And you should rise up to say you "deserve it",

Try to come out of your comfort zone,
Explore knowledge from the unknown,
Dominating you has become a habit,
And you should rise up to say you "deserve it".

-S Preethi Evanchline

Priya B Singh

Priya Singh was born & brought up in Dewas, Madhya Pradesh. She's a proud daughter of her Father B.N.Singh (T.I.).She's completed Masters of Computer Science; she is a Former Educationist, Communication Trainer & Avid Reader.

To know more about her writing visit

* Email: scspriyasingh@gmail.com

* Insta Id: instant__thoughts_

The Night

While walking on the road amid night,
Seems like flying above the lights,
No one was around,
Silence filled surround,

My mind says nothing to worry,
But my heart hurry,
After that man be transformed,
From man to ghost is now formed,

Being afraid of the ghost,
Our soul is being lost,
In this wide ground,
Ghosts are chatting in a clear sound,

They tortures and gives you no rest,
They shattered you into small pieces
Without breath you remain down lying,
And they never leave you until dying.

-Priya B Singh

Rashika Sawarkar

Rasika Ramesh Vanuta Sawarkar is a writer from Nagpur. She is pursuing her medical studies. She started writing from her childhood. She believes in kindness.

To know more about her writing visit

- ❖ Email: rasikasawarkar786@gmail.com

- ❖ Insta Id: @rasika_sawarkar

Her

People don't understand our suffering,
They tell god has given you ill fate offering,
And judge us from our clothes and flaws.
Do divert without asking about the cause.

They blames on our dressing sense,
And speak at our back as nonsense,
The supporters of the crime is hidden,
Truth is now forbidden,

Let us leave the ego,
And say to them 'no',
Not just the black and white face racism,
But men and women are too facing it,

Everyone says how a woman must be,
Teach a man how to be though he disagree,
They said we got independence earlier,
Still woman are fighting as a brave warrior,

Was that only for men?
When will our independence begin?

Do they only have the right to walk at night?
When will women's freedom enter with light?

With some hope in my heart,
I have come to take part,
In the struggle of every girl,
A man takes part like a pearl.

-Rasika Sawarkar

Sabtecah Beldazer A

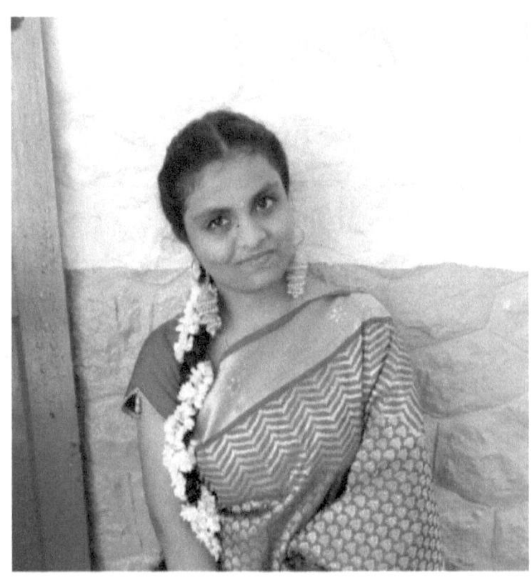

She is a twenty year old literature student with fierce enthusiasm in literature and writing is her passion.

To know more about her writing visit

- ❖   Email: sabtecahbeldazar@gmail.com

- ❖   Insta Id: sabtecah_beldazar

Rise up

Have no light?

Hope for the twilight,

Burnt art thou wound?

Make thyself a boon,

Terrified art thou noise?

Yell up thy voice,

Scars everywhere?

Don't let you down there,

Painful art thou ovaries?

Give your best berries,

Think you are a waste?

Lady, make your haste,

Book Benchers
Begin to end?

Make it and,

Lower art thou chin?

A lady is born to win,

-Sabtecah Beldazar A

Sevell L Fernandes

Sewell Lanisha Fernandes also known as Vier and Sidd. Born on 1st October 2002 in Goa, India is an Indian born Multilanguage author and poet. And she is an IOTA Athlete. She is also involved in music and Drama affairs and drawing, painting are her hobbies. She is also known for her street fashion style and she tends to live a simple life.

To know more about her writing visit

❖ Email: sewellfernandes@gmail.com

❖ Insta id: @sidd.vier

The lies forbidden

Afraid of the tomorrow days,

They fought thinking it is the only way,

And achieved for what they fought,

But the circumstance is constant,

Feeling as if they gained something,

We remain swimming with the tiny fins,

Moving behind the other fishes,

We lost our wishes,

Our happiness is being lost,

And everything is calculated into cost,

Without asking question,

We are being caught at the session,

In the hands of the fisherman,

Forgetting about our span,

As a fish we lost our lives,

In front of his sights we strive.

- Sevell L Fernandes

Suganthi s

Suganthi has been writing for over two years. She provides philosophical writings. Her educational background in English literature has given her a broad base for writings. Her books are available in Amazon Kindle named Heartly Sayings and Healing journey-11

To know more about her writing visit

❖ Email: ssuganthishunmugam@gmail.com

❖ Insta id: chum_moon

SHE

She looked after her children,

And they called her useless.

Earned for her children's mission,

Though they are homeless,

They called her a bad mother.

Though she strive forever,

She wore a skirt,

The society looks at her awkward,

And they called her shameless,

Regarded her as a mess,

She wore the burqa,

And also the burka,

They stopped her from entering temples,

But she is a perfect example,

And they questioned her womanhood,

Comparing her with the good,

Her life is filled with mystery,

Everyone questioned her history,

Sacrificing her life for her child,

Yet society never stopped talking wild.

-Suganthi. S

Sunita Bajaj

Presenting Sunita Bajaj, a housewife, dancer, yoga enthusiast, poet, writer, blogger and what not! She has been a co-author for more than 150 books including, the swings of life my queen.

To know more about her writing visit

- ❖ Email: sunitabajaj140774@gmail.com
- ❖ Insta Id: @abhivyakti_kuch_lafz

The Pain of a falling leaf

The pain of a falling leaf,

Has neither hope nor belief,

Every woman can understand that pain,

The travel to her husband's house in vain,

I left my parents who was tender,

The society treat us beggar,

It seems as if we are scattered,

Like the leaves of a tree that we watered

The branches are now broken,

New leaves be like a powerful slogan,

That makes that barren tree green again,

We wrap ourselves for the freedom to attain,

And makes it her second home,

She is locked in her room,

Falling leaves in autumn is a law of nature,

But we will never let it happen in the future.

-Sunita Bajaj

Supriya C.S.K

As a Co-author, Supriya is a good writer from Chennai. She has completed her graduation in commerce stream. She has been writing poetry for more than six months as her passion. She wants to be an entrepreneur in the future.

To know more about her writing visit

- Email: csksupriya15081998@gmail.com

A cry of a girl

Never harass a girl then her future ends,

For she cares you as her friend,

She thinks for everyone's happiness,

Remember you Worship a goddess,

For she gives you healings,

Never depart a woman's motherly feelings,

For it will turn to wind that depart,

By your cruel crooked heart,

And with your deadly aspect,

Do not destroy your respect,

By transforming a innocent girl to weird,

She has the power to conquer the world,

A Weapon that is sharper than the sword,

Is nothing but a woman's powerful word!

-Supriya C S K

Sushma F

Sushma has completed her Bachelor's degree and is going to step towards her master degree that is MBA. Her dream in life is much wider. She wanders for her desires.

To know more about her writing visit

❖ Email: fspmore@gmail.com

Rise up again

Women take your Rights,

By lighting the lights,

To bring a change,

In this world of challenge,

If we be a paper though they burn us,

We will rise up from the ashes,

Like the phoenix does,

We will be reborn,

We will shine in the dark,

Though we are a troop,

Believing there is a new hope,

We look to embark.

-Sushma F

Suthamancharri

She is Suthamancharri, a dentist. She is an astrophile, orinthophile, thalasophile A nature lover an empath Her native is kanyakumari .

To know more about her writing visit

❖   Email: sutha74mancharri@gmail.com

❖   Instagram Id: sutha_mancharri_sm

Silent screams

I'd wish to explore everything,

But I was always forbidden,

I'd like to dance and sing,

But my dreams were always silently hidden,

Deep in me there are lot of desires,

But they were slept unspoken,

I had no courage to pour my heartaches,

Little does anyone cared, to fix the broken,

I need someone to hear out my pain,

Someone to share my thoughts and feelings;

Little does anyone cared, everything in vain,

The scars remain without healing,

I'm always jealous on guys,

Who'd roam everywhere they wish,

Little does my heart cries,

Hoping someone would understand my anguish.

- Suthamancharri

Triparna Biswas

Triparna Biswas is a passionate writer from Kolkata. She loves to write and draw. She wants to be an army or a professional famous writer in the future. She started writing professionally in this lockdown. She loves to help the needy ones.

To know more about her writing visit

❖ Email: triparnabiswas55@gmail.com

❖ Instagram Id: @ tipu__tipu

Girls

Yes, I am girl who knows to fight,

And, have the right to bright,

Only we girls, know how our life,

Is full of strife,

Try to treat us equal,

Recorded as a sequel,

We struggle in the hands of Men,

Close our mouth by telling you are women,

We cry and die,

We girls are not products to buy,

We girls want to fight,

For every feminine' s right,

                                        - Triparna Biswas

Short story

Beril Jebastin

Beril, is a literarian. She is an enthusiast and absorber of human emotions who puts them in words. She loves to produce works in simple language, making them easier for everyone to understand. Her writings reveal her creativity. She believes words have power and writing is a medicine.

To know more about her writing visit

❖ Email: berilsounthini@gmail.com

❖ Insta Id: @beril_jebastin

NO COMING BACK!

"There were so many rich girls wanting to marry my son but he chose you. In spite of telling him so many times, he wanted to marry you. It's been almost a year and even now your father is not able to give the remaining dowry". Saratha's voice was louder towards Geetha who sat on the sofa exhausted after returning from work. Geetha has been listening to the same dialogue all these months from her marriage. Many times she has moved out of the house but came back with her husband's request yet her mother-in-law has not changed. She got up and went inside frustrated. In a few minutes her husband Raj came home.

"You know I have never spoken a word against your mom. But she can't take it as an advantage to speak to me like this. Is she in poverty to torture me for the rest of the dowry? Doesn't she know my family situation? My brother is getting married next month and I am bearing half the marriage expenses from my salary and not even yours. Can't she even wait? Where are we going to run away with giving the dowry?" Geetha poured out all her feelings in front of Raj. She continued, "I have my own self dignity and just can't listen to anybody talking about my family in a way that your mother does".

"I do understand your feelings Geetha but I cannot blindly trust your words just like that. And I know my mom has a louder voice but she will not speak as you portray her. I know my mom more than you." Raj replied and left the room. Geetha has never spoken disrespectfully to her mother-in-law and every time she spoke ill of Geetha's family, she spoke to her husband about this. Though she was very irritated with her behaviour, she thought it was right to talk to her husband about everything.

But when she realised that it was useless telling him, she decided what she had to do next. Geetha took her suitcase and packed her clothes. Sitting in the hall and listening to the sound, Saratha and Raj knew that she was packing to leave the house. When Geetha came out of her room and reached the main door, she stopped to look at them. "While my dad has taught me patience and discipline, he has taught me what self dignity is too. Have you eaten good food? In case you want to, visit my brother's marriage that is happening next month without getting even a single rupee from the bride". Saratha and Raj felt that place was hot with Geetha's emotions. They thought she would come back as usual but they didn't know that when a woman leaves someone for herself, there is no coming back.

-     Beril Jebastin

Krupali Makwana

She lives in India's first world heritage city. She is a law student and practicing lawyer at city civil and sessions court. I am a stenographer too.

To know more about her writing visit

❖ Insta handled: @ lmkrupali_

❖ Email: krupalimakwana2@gmail.com

The Crying Baby

On 18 January 2014, I was in my school days to be honest I was so jolly and a comedian of my class. That day I was wandering in my school washroom suddenly; I heard the voice of sobbing. The primary school girl, aged eleven years old, was crying. I was eager to go to her and asked why she was crying? She ignored me and tried to go but she was looking so pitiful so I let her go and next day she was crying again in the bathroom and I caught her so this time I have decided that no matter what may happen I will find out what would have happened to her. So this time I asked her politely but as usual I have to put more effort so I promised her to not tell anyone about this. So that the eleven year old girl confessed that her bus-driver was trying to touch her in a filthy way and suddenly she hugged me and cried so loud. At that time even I was so scared that he could misbehave with a little girl. And suddenly I saw her face. She was looking so helpless. And then I asked does anyone know about this? She replied no. So I told her to tell her mother so she denied it because of fear, I explained to her to be calm and go to her class. Then I met her teacher and told about this incident. Her teacher called her mother and explained this sensitive situation. Her mother was literally crying that her little girl was going through this kind of situation. But she told me not to tell anyone and just forget about her and this incident. At that time I thought how can she be so rude to her child? And she was worrying that if someone would know about this they'll lose their prestige. Before a mother, she is a woman who must have to know about this situation. After that incident the little girl named Khushi left the school and moved nearly to her home. And that incident changed my life and I questioned myself "Is being harassed a thing to ignore?

What will I do? Then I replied to myself I will never step back with these things. I will raise my voice more effectively than if I choose to be a lawyer and now I'm on my way.

- Krupali Makwan

Nanthini R

Nanthini is a 21 year old girl. She is an art's student. She is from Muhilan Vilai, Nagercoil.

To know more about her writing visit

❖ Email: nanthiniraja519@gmail.com

❖ Insta handled: @nanthini_rajasekhar

Mud Dauber

Once upon a time in the 1920's there lived a girl named Anna Lekshmi in India. She was married to Rathuna Lingam who was in his 40's while she was only 12 years old. When she didn't even know what life was. She enjoyed her wedding by wearing new dresses and eating Rasagulla, Jillebies, and Gulab Jamuns. She had two Elder sisters and a brother who were already married. She was even told by her father that Gandhi was married when he was 13 years old.

 She was very happy that she was going to be married before Gandhi got married. She got married that day. Her parents took her to her husband's house with some clothes, a golden chain and a bicycle for her husband. He doesn't know how to ride it. But her happiness disappeared on her wedding night as her husband sexually abused her.

As a child she didn't even know what was happening. She became a whole time house maid. A year passes, and her husband starts to worry that his 13 year old wife is not pregnant. He started to drink alcohol and started to abuse her each and every night. She even tried to run away from her husband's house. But her parents don't accept her. They even told her that she won't belong to her parent's house after she is married. She became a guest there and a person who makes her husband's wishes real at her husband's house.

At the age of sixteen she got pregnant. She was allowed to stay at her mother's house at that time. Her condition became critical. She was hospitalized. There she gave birth to twin girls before the due date. By keeping it as a reason her husband told her that those children are not born to him. In order to ignore those two girls, she became mentally weak and left her husband's house without a penny. There is no place for her at her mother's house , as her brother feared that he had to feed her family throughout his life. She became homeless, and ended up in the streets. She starts to work under a landlord to feed her children.

Time passes, she builds a small hut for her and her children to live, and they live happily. But it does not last long. Her landlord forced her to give the land to him which she earned using her past seven year savings. Tears, sadness, and her wounded heart became her only companion. With some little hope in heart they might have a happy life, then one night after some months have passed she started a small company and step by step it developed and finally she reached a great height. The twin girls later owned the company and one day they saw their father wearing a torn dress and were begging in the street. When they saw it their heart sank and the father realized his mistakes and they took him to home and lived prosperously.

-Nanthini R

Sananshika Malik

Sananshika Malik is an Indian writer, author and founder of _the stunning_ Compiler_ Company. She started her writing career at the age of 19. She has completed over 40+ books at the age of just 19 and got a national record Holder by Anand Shree Organization too.

To know more about her writing visit

- ❖   Insta handled: Maliksananshika_

- ❖   Email: maliksananshika15@gmail.com

The Fake Feminism World

There is a moment when Sia and her family get happy where Sia used to be father's angel. Sia was an elder daughter of her house and then two of her sisters and then her younger brother. Everything seems to be happy, everything seems to be exciting. Her Papa comes to the house every night early and has a lot of gifts in his hand. They as children went so quickly and met their father so excitingly.

Their mother used to cook for them. They just waited for their yummy hungry food on their tummy. Every night they used to sleep for their dreamy dream books. And then later they woke up in a happy mood and went to school with their father's car. But one day something happened which shocked their house harshly. Her Papa went to god place and after one month they all lost our younger brother too.

It was a harsh moment for them. Their mother is still facing a traumatized problem, she used to be in depression while thinking of her past. Sia has to leave her study for her mother's care. Without any education Sia and her younger sister went to another house as a house maid. They earn money from that job and take food for their living. As women had no one to help them for their safety they kept dogs to protect themselves. As an elder child Sia had to marry early and her dream of becoming a doctor broke sooner.

After that one day everything ruined, many problems were going on in her life and now something happened which broke her entire family. Her landlord, along with Sia and her family, threw them out of the house, locking the dogs that used to protect them and locked them in the same house. In the rain, Sia and her family kept on weeping on the sidewalk, and the dogs kept crying in the house inside her hut, hungry and thirsty to come back.

 No one came to help them even the police officer took bribes for the rich people and just because of facing poverty Sia and her family can't do anything. But as a matter of feminism no one gives sia an opportunity to prove herself . People just wanted to know why more happened to them so that they would gossip about it. As a matter of feminism no one stands with sia and her family. People who talked about feminism are now just wondering about what will happen next to their family ? A FAKE FEMINISM WORLD

-Sananshika Malik

Sapna P

She is SAPNA PARASURAMAN born on 30.04.2003 in Pondicherry, India. A lover of Arts and Literature, a student of B.A.English Literature at BISHOP HEBER COLLEGE, TRICHY , TAMILNADU, INDIA.She is an All - Rounder. She was the one day RJ of Suriyan F.M 93.5, Pondicherry. She secured 3rd place in Interschool Badminton Competition which was conducted by Pondicherry government. She is a good human being with humanity and helping tendency.She likes to shine and has a selfless- mind . She is very passionate in all her works," Cool in heart, Chill in mind , makes her Character , a spicy one ".She is very amicable and she would never put her dreams down. She is a co-author for more than fifteen

books. She is also a NSS VOLUNTEER of Bishop Heber College,Trichy,Tamilnadu.

To know more about her writing visit

❖ Insta handled: @ sapnadeebika
❖ Email: sapnaparasuraman@gmail.com

Honour the feminine

Women are the real representatives of society. She has learnt physical courage by facing molestation and eve teasing and mental courage through gender politics and male domination. She is the root of this society, without SHE no more HE. Basically, He is the dependent of She; But people have changed it and made them as their homemaker. Every time the decisions are taken only by men, at last only it will reach women along with their answers. Do this is the space they have given to them?, they themselves decided it as right or wrong; but for their reputation in society, they would confess that," OFTEN OUR DECISIONS WILL BE THE SAME ".

"OUR WOMEN IN HOME ALSO HAVE THE RIGHTS TO TAKE DECISIONS" ,was actually flopped up. Do the men have prepared the dinner before 8 am? Do the men have assigned the family budget? Do the men have spent some quality time with their son and daughter?. All the men are free from their family responsibilities; because, all women have sacrificed their dreams and career and done only with floor cleaning, vessel washing, sweeping, ironing, finally the lavatory cleaning. Till evening, they don't spare time for their nap. It was the auspicious time to prepare the delicious snacks for her son, daughter, husband, father-in-law, mother-in-law. During festival time she is an all- Rounder like an electric current with full time of energy to work.

" ENCUMBRANCE TO EMANCIPATION WILL PROGRESS SOON "

Likewise, Does she pour his anger on family members? Does she have any weekend? Do the family men have cooked for all the days? Have the family men visited to clean the lavatory at once?. Majority of the answers will be "NO". Because the basic mentality of the boys is " Girls are weaker, silly crier, sentimental fools". The mentality of the men is "All women want to work under the guidance of men, No more decision making by their own, First preference is only for men, After men have finished their food only women want to eat ". This is the space they have given to women. Women are an integral part of each one of our lives. When we become old, we will understand the values of our women. But that time, they would not be there to pacify our tears.

"I BELIEVE, BELIEVE, BELIEVE....

ONE DAY,OUR SOCIETY WILL BE ACTIVE

WITH GENDER EQUALITY

WITHOUT GENDER DISCRIMINATION "

-Sapna P

Tushar R

Tushar. R is an aspiring writer. He writes quotes and poems in English. He works on his hobbies like playing tennis and reading books. The two lockdowns gave him a kick start to his ideas. He also posts his writings on his Instagram page @breaking_maturity .His writing habit gives him strength, belief, and confidence in his life. He has a vast interest in creating a better world through his writings. Tushar loves to evolve and hence his writings would convey a good message to the world.

To know more about his writing visit

❖ Email: tusharr.thoughts@gmail.com

❖ Instagram Id: @tusharr_4

Actress and feminism

The teen girl who matured recently in a village experienced mixed emotions all at the same time. She always wanted to become a theatre artist. Eventually, her goal was to become a famous actress. Her family never believed her. They took away her dreams by restricting her always. She was Nidhi, a 16-year-old girl from a remote village, Hampapura. She had the charm on her face and her voice was too good. She was even one of the prayers lead at her school. Her voice was too good. Like all girls, she too experienced love in her imagination. Nidhi was a normal girl with extraordinary skills which many of them never noticed. Her voice was her power.

After her schooling, she was admitted to a college in Mysore city, where she went up and down every day by bus. Her eyes went on those big posters of actresses advertising products, all over the city. She felt what she wanted to be. She researches and finds out the famous theatre to become an artist. With her studies, she manages to take classes at Kalamandir. Nidhi always pays her fee with the money she saved from the bus ticket where she used to walk a few miles just to save up some money. She manages to collect money for her fees. At one point she breaks her piggy bank which was filled with coins and notes to pay her fees. Her acting skills improved gradually with time.

After a good ranking in the Engineering entrance exam, she manages to get a free seat in the government engineering college in the same city. She wanted much more time to shine in the theatre. She shined one day when the whole show was lightened by her performance. A film director was the chief guest and appreciated her and gave her an offer for a short film.

She made it trending on YouTube with her performance. She performed as a poor girl who thrived to be a successful girl through farming. She got appreciation from all over India. She approached many directors after her film but many of them ignored helping her as she was an independent artist with no wealthy background. Many of the directors invited her to their home giving the reason for an audition but they sexually harassed her and made her image filled with scars. Her dark complexion made many directors simply reject her without even an audition. She was traumatized by these experiences but her mother always motivates her. She took a break from the film industry for two years.

In villages, you cannot judge a person who is mentally ill because they don't know about the care we should give for our mental health. Many small girls are made to marry without thinking about their mental abuse which the husband may cause her and force her to do all the work without any rest for her. Nidhi's burning desire never stopped her. She created short films with very good scripts written by her. Her friends who were technically good from Mysore helped her to make short films on feminism, rape accused girl's life and on dowry system too. She grew independently and she became famous on YouTube. The director who once rejected her takes an appointment with her PA to meet her. With her name, her village too became famous as she set up her office in her village to let people remember her name with her village's name as her surname, Nidhi Hampapura.

-Tushar R